NAPALM
COCKTAILS

SKETCHES FROM THE OTHER SIDE OF MY SOUL

VOLUME FIFTEEN

NAPALM
COCKTAILS

SKETCHES FROM THE OTHER SIDE OF MY SOUL

VOLUME FIFTEEN

V. A. MATATUMUA VERMEULEN

Napalm Cocktails. Sketches from the Other Side of My Soul, Volume Fifteen.
© 1994-2020 Vincent A. Matatumua Vermeulen also known as Vincent Albert Vermeulen.

Published by Hyacinthus Books™ an imprint of Island Ink Publishing Co. Ltd. 71-75 Shelton Street, Covent Garden, London, WC2H 9JQ, United Kingdom.

ISBN-13: 978-1-914093-23-4

A CIP catalogue record for this book is available from the British Library.

Names: Matatumua Vermeulen, Vincent Albert also known as Vermeulen, Vincent Albert 1969 – author

Title: Napalm Cocktails Sketches from the Other Side of My Soul, Volume Fifteen | Vincent Albert Matatumua Vermeulen also known as Vincent Albert Vermeulen

Subjects: BISAC: POE 021000 POETRY / LGBT, POE023010 POETRY / Subjects & Themes / Death, Grief, Loss, POE023020 POETRY / Subjects & Themes / Love & Erotica, POE 010000 POETRY/ Australia & Oceania.

Napalm Cocktails is dedicated to my God Apollo Musagetes as well as to Eros, Anteros, Himeros and Pothos.

Napalm Cocktails is also dedicated to Derick Camarigg, thanks for the dance; to Vincent Gerrard Motos sorry about the tie; Martin Saker, because.

A che più debb'io mai l'intensia voglia

A che più debb'io mai l'intensa voglia
Sfogar con pianti o con parole meste,
Se di tal sorte 'l ciel, che l'alma veste,
Tard' o per tempo, alcun mai non ne spoglia?
A che 'l cor lass' a più morir m'invoglia,
S'altri pur dee morir? ...

Why should I seek to pacify intense desire
With bitter tears and empty words of grief,
When neither soon nor late heaven send relief
To souls that love elect surrounds with fire?
Why should my aching heart to death aspire
When all must die? ....

Michelangelo Buonarroti.

CONTENTS

NAPALM
COCKTAILS

SKETCHES FROM THE OTHER SIDE OF MY SOUL

VOLUME FIFTEEN

1: GONE

gone -
out of my life
before i could know you
why then
do i ache
with an emptiness
i knew not possible
for eyes
that touched my soul
gently
too kindly
your lips brushed mine
and you held me
briefly
but fondly
i like to believe
for my parting gift
of words
inscribed so plainly
revealing my heart
and its lost cause
to you
as i held you tightly
wishing so hard
it hurt

01/09/94 (to Deric Camarigg).

1

2: REMEMBER ME?

i think of you
walking
the streets of L.A.
with all those handsome men
to beguile you
and wonder –
will you remember
some young fool
whose heart
was given to you
on a scrap of parchment?

01/09/94 (to Deric Camarigg).

3: PRESUMPTION

i fall
too easily
for divinity
'tis my curse
no doubt
for my presumption
of hoping
to be worthy
of such a lover
as you

01/09/94 (to Deric Camarigg).

4. COUNTRY DANCING

your eyes
bespelled me
two stepping
face to face
i don't even like
country dancing
being a Strauss man
myself
but for you
i did
- with you
. . .
i loved it

03/09/94. (to Deric Camarigg).

5: ENDLESS

the days
are endless
and nights
stretch forever
empty
cold and pale
lifeless
but for your image
engraved in my heart
for all eternity

03/09/94 (for Martin Saker)

6: ON THE WINGS OF YOUR SMILE

your eyes
do not burn
my soul
nor would i
drown in them
for yours
are gentle eyes
soft and smiling
they lift me
unto the stars
which float in them
as i do
a moonbeam light
hawk-swift free
i swoop
exhilarated
on the wings of your smile

03/09/94. (to Deric Camarigg).

7: MY HEART

you held
my heart
in the palm of your hand
and knew it not
all the while
it lay beating
quietly –
fearful
you would notice
how intensely
it needed you
to notice it

03/09/94. (to Deric Camarigg).

8: WOLF HEART

wolf heart
why weep
and howl
your soul dry
each night
beneath the golden moon
that you
could never reach

05/09/94.

9: DAEMON HEART

wail –
oh daemon heart
for all you wish
could be
or, had been
yet –
never will
nor was
[ever]

05/09/94.

10: TIME

life passes
like autumn leaves
and
so soon
the tree is bare

18/09/94.

11: STRANGE FIEND

some strange fiend
you must be
that our paths cross
so often
but never meet
our eyes touching
lingering
hinting, promises
but ever distant
. . . distant

15/10/94.

12: NAKED EARTH

naked earth
you flaunt yourself
shamelessly
unlike
those foolish creations
who hide their forms
so shamefully

17/10/94.

13: ODE TO THE GUM TREE

Oh naked gums
ye ethereal armies
of spirit sentinels
standing silent
beneath
an indigo
midnight clear
How
can ye call me
across the great Gulf
Am i
but one of thee
alone
lost and wandering
the endless vastness (beyond)
yearning
to be
with thee

19/10/04.

14: SHOULD DRAGONS FLY

Should dragons fly
across the pregnant moon
blooming golden
to carry me
across the silver mirror sea
and the sisters three
whose fulsome peaks
hold aloft
the ebony pearly sky
'twould be
in search of you
astride a mighty steed
of dazzling white
in shining armour bright
to do battle
great and fierce
i, in mage robes dark
to win your soul
or give you mine
anyway

19/09/94 (to Dcric Camarigg).

15: QUEST

'twas once
upon a midnight sea
when all but foaming dancing gilded waves
did sleep
beneath the feathery mist
of the fairy silver moon
there sailed a questor true
for perilous distant shores
enchanted child of ancient magic
forsaken foundling of elven blood
vision quested
he sought his destiny:
a prince divine
who rode a dragon steed
and sailed the sun

24/10/94

16: BLOODY VESTMENTS

dark the sun shall burn
over the bloody vestments
of my sacrifice
and my riven soul
shall burst free
from its prison
cursing it
and all
who confined it so
free at last
to ride the ether
in wild abandon
eternal . . .

25/10/94.

17: EMPTINESS

I have an emptiness
if only they knew
my passion . . .
my love . . .
for –
they would fear me
curse me perhaps
thinking they
were prey
 . . .
what if they were?

25/10/94.

18: YESTERDAY'S HORIZONS

the evening skies
glow bitter
acid sunsets
drip
upon ravaged seas
yesterdays' horizons
but memories
now . . .

29/10/94.

19: NAPALM COCKTAILS

napalm cocktails
strip my mind
of all
but the blitzkrieg music
assaulting me
and the gyrating bodies
twisting in the blinding strobes
screaming soundlessly
for me –
to join them

29/10/94.

20: RECONNAISSANCE

our eyes
playing cat and mouse
are you?
aren't you
we ask
fugitively casting
telepathic signals
that we do not
act upon
hoping only
that further reconnaissance
will verify
what we already know

29/10/94.

21: DRAGON HEART

little dragon heart
you sweep
you dust
in endless drudgery
longing so achingly
to fly the vaulting skies

shake loose
the kinks in your wings
and cast up your eyes
to the great vastness
that beckons

fantastic voyages
from star to star
separated only
by space
waiting
for the wingbeats
of your heart

cast aside
that duster and broom
leap up, fly away
into the vast beyond
that waits
to embrace you
in its eternity

30/10/94.

22: THE OCEAN

blinding silver
the blazing sea does shine
with merciless splendour
Vibrant extravagance
is Poseidon's majesty

30/10/94.

23: VIOLET MIND

cry, cry
oh violet mind
nebulous
are your songs
floating; vaporous
in the silvery sky
shadows dark
they swirl
dancing sinuously
among whispering moonbeams

04/11/94

24: ETCH ME A SONG

dip your claw
in my soul
and etch me a song
dark
as the heart
that bled it
one of ancient power
so great
They could never
destroy it
even
the fiercest flames
eternal
sing of light
so bright
it is utter darkness
of Joy
so intense
no agony
can match it
with my blood
i bid you

write −

of Love

05/11/94.

25: SHORES OF TIME

The shores of time
are finest sand
slipping through fingers
even as we valiantly try
to build castles
on the shifting shores of time

09/11/94.

26: I DON'T KNOW WHY

You are an angel
i
i am nothing
Why did you enter my life
Angel that you are
i know nothing
i want nothing else
But you
You are all i want
And need
But i
do not know
Why

12/11/94 (pour V.G.M.).

27: SUBTLY

you conquered me
so subtly
i know not how
but that you did
and would not
that you had not

12/11/94 (to V.G.M.).

28: THE GODS

the gods
must have some malicious plan
throwing me
in your path
such wondrous fortune
i doubt –
knowing too well
their fickle nature
and cruel humour
thus, i fear
you may not love me
or worse
that you do
and so be taken from me
as they will . . .
in jest

12/11/94 (to V.G.M.).

29: TOO EASILY

i fall too easily
like some fool
i cast my heart
before a stranger's feet
but is it foolishness
to hope . . .?

12/11/94.

30: I CALLED YOU

i called you
to ask you
if you'd seen my heart
for it followed you home
last night
leaving me alone
cold and miserable
wondering
if i'd see you again
i know not
and dare not hope
so if you hear it
panting in haste
to follow you
or see its whirlwind
wagging tail
so ecstatic
to be near you
look after it
will you not
for it chooses
its own master
and too long ago
i lost that claim

12/11/94 (to V.G.M.).

31: LIGHTNING STRUCK

I've been struck by lightning
And now
I don't know anything
But you

12/11/94 (pour V.G.M.)

32: BE REAL

we are so newly met
and yet . . .
my whole being
aches for you
your voice to caress me
your presence
flings my soul beyond the stars
in wild abandon
touch me . . .
i would be yours
eternally
how can this be?
what sweet madness
has touched me?
i am terrified
this is but a dream
and you . . .
please,
please be real

12/11/94 (to V.G.M.)

ACKNOWLEDGEMENTS

I'd like to thank all those who read *Napalm Cocktails* during its compilation and preparation for publication, especially those who read my other "sketches" during the early years while I was a student at James Cook University and encouraged me to keep writing and the very few who read my work after I left finished my undergraduate degree there.

In particular I'd like to give special thanks to: Adriana Peters, Clem Matheson and Wade J. Mullings for being my flat mates and best frinds at Uni and; Fiona Shon, Catherine Cantarella and Ludmilla Solonda for reading my poetry over cappuccino with fish and chips between French lectures at James Cook University; Jason Russo, Jacqui Garza, Joe Meyers, Pearce Nelson, Dayan Cronin and Rhonda Veivers for reading; Belinda Rose Veivers for writing a poem about me and reading my poetry and attempts at science fiction and fantasy; and Rey Ileto for saying he's never had a "Poet" in one of his classes before.

I also want to thank Jayson Bebrouth for his interest and encouragement of my publication efforts as well as Fiti Leung Wai, Charlotte Chan Mow and Jerry Brunt for their interest and encouragement.

Thanks also to: Brenda Latu-Heather for reading and sharing my poetry with others in the Attorney General's Office and telling them I was a poet; Vincent L. Fasone Jr. for restoring my faith in the innate kindness and goodness of people and being kind and generous to strangers in distress as well as for his moral support, kindness and friendship, over the years and Joe Meyers for reading my poems and commissioning one from me as well as letting me stay with his family in Mililani, Hawaii.

I also want to thank: Mrs Sue Rasmussen for reading my very early attempts at science fiction and fantasy and for encouraging me to write, way back when I was still in high school, even though she was not my teacher; my English teachers at Samoa College and the National University of Samoa: Miss VandenDriesen, Mrs Kolose, Mrs Beverly Barlow, Mrs. Emma Kruse-Vaai and Mrs Sina Vaai.

I would also like to thank Laulu Lolesio Tevaga, the Government Printer for his patience and taking the time to answer my questions about the offset printing process and preparation of print ready masters and esoteric things like margins even though I was only supposed to be following up on the status of the printing of the government's budget documents and not be getting an introduction to the offset printing process. Likewise I must thank Makerita Vaai of the University of the South Pacific's Malifa Library and Mataina Te'o of the Nelson Memorial Library who were helpful in my very early efforts to learn about copyright law and the publication process when I was at Leif'ifi Intermediate and Samoan College. Mataina also rescued me from spending a weekend locked in the library.

I must also thank: Mrs Lynne Enari and my aunt Christine Quested for offering advice on what to include in the "About the author" section; Claire Lepack and Sonny Mulitalo for their advice on how to resolve certain bank conundrums that were proving an obstacle to being able to set things up for Island Ink Publishing to be able to start publishing; my cousins Hinauri Petana and Unutoa Auelua for confirming Laulu, Makerita and Mataina's full names for me and Caroline Applin for the chocolates and Monte Carlos sent to Belgium all the way from Australia.

I would also like to acknowledge and give special thanks to my aunt and uncle: Jan and Tom Reyes as well as one of my best friends and former flatmate: Wade J. Mullings for their financial assistance without which the publication of this book would not have been possible. Thank you so much. I really appreciate your support and faith in me.

I must also thank the late Ms Mable Howse of Leifi'ifi Intermediate School for introducing me to writing poetry. You planted a seed long ago and I am sad that you did not get to see its flowering let alone its fruits.

And James Barnes, Dean Taylor, Martin Saker and Brett Page: for just being.

Blessed Be.

Vincent A. Matatumua Vermeulen,

Brussels, BELGIUM

ABOUT THE POET

Born in Hawaii, Vincent A. Matatumua Vermeulen also known as Vincent A. Vermeulen grew up in Samoa. His education began at Saint Theresa's Catholic School and was continued briefly in Belgium and the United Kingdom. Upon returning to Samoa he completed his primary and secondary education at Apia Primary School, Leifiifi Intermediate School and Samoa College.

He commenced his tertiary studies at the National University of Samoa where he completed his University Preparatory Certificate and was awarded an AusAid Scholarship to study at James Cook University in Townsville, Queensland, Australia.

Following the completion of a Bachelor of Arts degree in Australia he commenced working in the Samoan Civil Service first in the Treasury/Ministry of Finance and then in the Ministry of Foreign Affairs and Trade, leaving occasionally to live in Hawaii as well as to pursue postgraduate studies at the University of Sydney in New South Wales, Australia, the Katholike Universiteit Leuven in Flemish Brabant, Belgium and the University of Bristol, England in the United Kingdom.

From a young age Vincent grew to love reading, so much that he was became a regular visitor at the Nelson Memorial Library in Apia and often was given special dispensation to stay in the children's section in the mezzanine after the Children's section closed. This led to him getting accidentally locked into the Library one Friday evening when librarians forgot he was there. His introduction to the writing of poetry was at Leifiifi Intermediate School through his English Teacher the late redoubtable Ms Mable Howse. However, although he did write a few poems that were published in the Samoa College News Bulletin, it was not until at James Cook University that he started writing poetry in earnest. He had some poetry selections (along with some articles on history and politics) published in the Magnus Taurus and others in The Orphean.

NOTES TO THIS EDITION

This is the first edition of *Napalm Cocktail,* the fifteenth volume of *Sketches from the Other Side of My Soul* which currently comprises twenty one completed volumes of poetry. *Napalm Cocktails* covers a period from September 1994 to November 1994. However, this edition contains some changes to the form of the poetry. These changes reflect some of the changes that I made during compilation of *Dragon Waif, A Selection of Sketches from the Other Side of My Soul*.

Perhaps one of the most significant has been the inclusion of titles. Although I originally started using titles I abandoned their use half way through *Empty Wells*, the second volume of *Sketches from the Other Side of My Soul*. Latter I designated roman numerals to each poem prefixed by the volume number based on the order that they had been written in. I have decided to do away with the numbering and reinstitute titles.

I also ceased to use capitals except in very specific instances. This was because to me a capital letter indicated the start of a new sentence. The problem that I saw with this was that in some cases depending on how one read them, there were poems in which one could actually read (for example) line one and two as a complete sentence as well as line two and three and in the same sense line three and four, all as separate sentences. That is lines one to four could not be read as one sentence but each line could in some way form part of the preceding or subsequent line. I felt at the time that capitals would preclude the ability of readers to see and appreciate this.

Another important reason for my decision to not use capitals was because of the letter 'i'. By using a small "i" for the personal pronoun I was seeking to impart a sense of diminishing the importance of the self as in the self, had become so diminished that it no longer merited a capital letter. This aspect has been retained to the chagrin of the spell check program. One factor which made me reconsider the lack of capitals is that someone assumed that I was imitating e. e.

cummings and I did not appreciate that assumption. Not because I do not like e. e. cummings but because I do not like the thought of anyone assuming I was copying someone else's style. I recognise that this is a logical if incorrect assumption but although I capitalized the letters of each line in *Dragon Waif* I decided to just leave things as they are for most of the poems because it was simpler to do so and reflected the original structure of the poems.

I have however, made some changes to the wording of some poems as well as changing their structure to some extent. Some of this has been due to trying to fit some poems onto a page. However, I tried to refrain as much as possible from too much editing as I have always felt that in the case of these poems that the original flow of thoughts and words had been captured in the form most reflective of the thoughts and emotions that generated them.

As with Dragon Waif I debated including illustration. This was in part to generate more white space which advisors on preparing volumes of poetry indicate is important in designing a book of poetry. This is why many books of poetry have poems only on one page faced by an illustration or a blank page. The other reason that I considered including illustrations is to ensure that poems that extended over two pages would end up opening up side by side rather than on different sides of the same leaf. I could have shuffled poems about to ensure that this happened but wanted to retain the order in which they were written.

Although this chronological order was to an extent broken or rendered irrelevant in Dragon Waif since it was composed of a selection of poems made from the first fifteen volumes of Sketches from the Other side of My Soul and as such the chronology is skewed as interposing poems are missing. In this and all the other volumes the chronological order is retained. Although I am not sure if this will be of any interest or provide any insight to anyone.

One other major change is that of the name under which this and all the other volumes are published under. Originally I had wanted to use the pseudonym Nikolai Alexsandrov as the pen name under which to publish my poetry. In the end I settled on Darum which is what is on the cover of the 1st and 2nd lot of chapbooks of *Dragon Waif* which I gave out to some friends and relatives in 1995 and 2002.

Part of the reason behind my wanting to use a pseudonym is that there are many very dark poems throughout all of my work. That is poems dealing with death, depression and suicide. In addition there are a number love poems that I was worried about how people would react negatively to.

This edition is published under the my real name Vincent A. Matatumua Vermeulen. I was going to publish it under the shorter Vincent A. Vermeulen which I am also know by rather than using the double barrelled surname which can cause confusion for some people. But while doing some searches for something else I discovered that there was already at least one author named Vincent Vermeulen.

So in order to avoid any confusion I've decided to publish under Vincent A. Matatumua Vermeulen which in order to fit on the book cover has been shortened to V. A. Matatumua Vermeulen on the cover. Incidentally while I was at James Cook University I published quite a few poems in the weekly *Bullsheet* as well as the monthly *Magnus Taurus*. All these were published under Vincent A. Matatumua Vermeulen, so this ensures both less confusion as well as some continuity.

ABOUT ISLAND INK PUBLISHING

Island Ink Publishing is a small independent publishing house. We publish poetry, including collections, pamphlets and the occasional anthology; fiction, including novels, novellas and collections of short stories; non-fiction, including history, law, botany, memoirs and travel writing; lexicons, including bilingual and multilingual dictionaries as well as phrasebooks and botanical lexicons; language acquisition material, including dual language texts, language learning books and other learning and teaching materials.

We also publish out of print classic and heritage works of academic, cultural, historical and literary importance, including fiction, non-fiction, poetry, lexicons and compilations of documents; and translations of various works, including classical and heritage works.

Island Ink Publishing Company Limited is also interested in finding and promoting new authors. We are especially interested in fiction by own voice authors especially, but not limited to authors of minority and marginalized communities. We are also interested in fiction portraying characters of minority and marginalized communities as protagonists and or major characters in strong positive role as well as works dealing with issues related to such communities.

Although we mainly publish books in English and French, we also publish books in other languages and are always seeking to extend our range of languages.

Please visit our website to find out more about us, what books we have available and what our submission guidelines are.

SKETCHES FROM THE OTHER SIDE OF MY SOUL

Sketches from the Other Side of My Soul currently comprises the following volumes:

Venusian Mysteries	Volume 1	1990-1991
Empty Wells	Volume 2	1992
Silver Velvet	Volume 3	1992
Stone Tower	Volume 4	1992
Mirror of My Soul	Volume 5	1992
Prince of Shadows	Volume 6	1992
Shadow Born	Volume 7	1992
Dark Eyes	Volume 8	1993
Adsum Domine	Volume 9	1993
Blood and Shadows	Volume 10	1993
Moth Heart	Volume 11	1993
Dark Orisons	Volume 12	1993
Dream Spinner	Volume 13	1994
Ice Lord	Volume 14	1994
Napalm Cocktails	Volume 15	1994-1995
Diamond Kisses	Volume 16	1995
Anemones in the Wind	Volume 17	1995-1996
Ashes	Volume 18	1996-1999
Like Icarus	Volume 19	2000
Dark Flight	Volume 20	2000-2020
Dark Eternity	Volume 21	2020 – 2021

OTHER WORKS BY THE AUTHOR

Dragon Waif. A Selection of Sketches from the Other Side of My Soul: comprised of selections from the first 15 Volumes of Sketches from the Other Side of My Soul.
ISBN - 978-1-914093-00-5 Paperback edition.
ISBN - 978-1-914093-01-2 Hard Cover edition.

Heart Ink. A Selection of Sketches from the Other Side of My Soul: comprised of selections from the first 20 Volumes of Sketches from the Other Side of My Soul.
ISBN - 978-1-914093-02-9 Paperback edition.
ISBN - 978-1-914093-03-6 Hard Cover edition.

Sketches from the Other Side of My Soul Volumes 1 – 5
ISBN - 978-1-914093-04-3 Hard Cover edition

Sketches from the Other Side of My Soul Volumes 6 – 10
ISBN - 978-1-914093-05-0 Hard Cover edition

Sketches from the Other Side of My Soul Volumes 11 – 15
ISBN - 978-1-914093-06-7 Hard Cover edition

Sketches from the Other Side of My Soul Volumes 16 – 20
ISBN - 978-1-914093-07-4 Hard Cover edition

Venusian Mysteries. Sketches from the Other Side of My Soul Volume 1
ISBN -978-1-914093-09-8 Paperback edition
Empty Wells. Sketches from the Other Side of My Soul Volume 2
ISBN - 978-1-914093-10-4 Paperback edition
Silver Velvet. Sketches from the Other Side of My Soul Volume 3
ISBN - 978-1-914093-11-1 Paperback edition
Stone Tower. Sketches from the Other Side of My Soul Volume 4
ISBN - 978-1-914093-12-8 Paperback edition
Mirror of My Soul. Sketches from the Other Side of My Soul Volume 5
ISBN - 978-1-914093-13-5 Paperback edition
Prince of Shadows. Sketches from the Other Side of My Soul Volume 6
ISBN - 978-1-914093-14-2 Paperback edition
Shadow Born. Sketches from the Other Side of My Soul Volume 7
ISBN - 978-1-914093-15-9 Paperback edition
Dark Eyes. Sketches from the Other Side of My Soul Volume 8
ISBN - 978-1-914093-16-6 Paperback edition
Adsum Domine. Sketches from the Other Side of My Soul Volume 9
ISBN - 978-1-914093-17-3Paperback edition
Blood and Shadows. Sketches from the Other Side of My Soul Volume 10
ISBN - 978-1-914093-18-0 Paperback edition
Moth Heart. Sketches from the Other Side of My Soul Volume 11
ISBN - 978-1-914093-19-7 Paperback edition
Dark Orisons. Sketches from the Other Side of My Soul Volume 12
ISBN - 978-1-914093-20-3 Paperback edition
Dream Spinner. Sketches from the Other Side of My Soul Volume 13
ISBN - 978-1-914093-21-0 Paperback edition
Ice Lord. Sketches from the Other Side of My Soul Volume 14
ISBN - 978-1-914093-22-7 Paperback edition
Napalm Cocktails. Sketches from the Other Side of My Soul Volume 15
ISBN - 978-1-914093-23-4 Paperback edition
Diamond Kisses. Sketches from the Other Side of My Soul Volume 16
ISBN - 978-1-914093-24-1 Paperback edition
Anemones in the Wind. Sketches from the Other Side of My Soul Volume 17
ISBN - 978-1-914093-25-8 Paperback edition
Ashes. Sketches from the Other Side of My Soul Volume 18
ISBN - 978-1-914093-26-5 Paperback edition
Like Icarus. Sketches from the Other Side of My Soul Volume 19
ISBN - 978-1-914093-27-2 Paperback edition
Dark Flight. Sketches from the Other Side of My Soul Volume 20
ISBN - 978-1-914093-28-9 Paperback edition
Dark Eternity. Sketches from the Other Side of My Soul Volume 21
ISBN - 978-1-914093-29-6 Paperback edition .

Published by Hyacinthus Books™ an imprint of
Island Ink Publishing Company Limited, 71-75 Shelton Street,
Covent Garden, London, WC2H 9JQ, UNITED KINGDOM
Typeset in Garamond 36 and 18 point.
Perpetua Titling MT 14 and 11 point
Calibri 11 point
Verdana 10 and 8 point
Typesetting, layout and design by Dioskouri Designs
Cover image www.Canva.com

Island Ink Publishing Co. Ltd.

Printed in Great Britain
by Amazon

33274465R00037